B. P. Pratten

The Canadian centennial Guide to New York and Philadelphia

B. P. Pratten

The Canadian centennial Guide to New York and Philadelphia

ISBN/EAN: 9783337148270

Printed in Europe, USA, Canada, Australia, Japan

Cover: Foto ©Lupo / pixelio.de

More available books at **www.hansebooks.com**

THE

CANADIAN

Centennial Guide

TO

NEW YORK AND PHILADELPHIA

BY

THIRTY DIFFERENT ROUTES,

CONTAINING A DETAILED STATEMENT OF EACH ROUTE, AND ITS
COST FROM EVERY LARGE TOWN IN CANADA.

BROCKVILLE:

LEAVITT AND SOUTHWORTH, PRINTERS,

1876

THE

CANADIAN CENTENNIAL GUIDE.

—

The information contained in the CANADIAN CENTENNIAL GUIDE, is of very great importance to those who contemplate a visit to the Centennial Exhibition the coming season. The pamphlet is compiled more for the special benefit of those who wish to have an accurate knowledge of the expense of the entire trip, before leaving home, than for the more favored to whom expense is of trifling consideration; and yet the latter will find in it information of much value, in the detailed description of the various routes, and the opportunity afforded of securing accommodations in advance, either in New York, or Philadelphia and its surroundings.

The objects sought to be attained by the GUIDE may be classified under several distinct headings, as follows : —

First.—To give a detailed description of the various Railroad and Steamboat Routes to Philadelphia and return, and their cost, from the principal railroad centres of Canada, and the American frontier.

Second.—To present the claims of each road from a business standpoint, and also as affording the greatest amount of pleasure on the trip.

Third.—To present a list of the hotels and boarding houses in Philadelphia and its surroundings, their locality, price of board per day and week, and accommodations ; together with a similar guide to New York, for the benefit of those who desire to spend a few days in the Metropolis, either going or returning.

Fourth.—A description of the points of interest in the two cities worthy of inspection, and the cheapest and most convenient methods of reaching them.

AN HISTORICAL SKETCH.

It will be interesting in this connection to know something of the history of the Centennial project, whose fulfillment was witnessed on the 10th of May last. It is utterly impossible to give the name of the first individual who first suggested the idea of a grand national celebration in commemoration of the Declaration of Independence. It was repeatedly alluded to in Fourth of July orations, and in editorials printed by leading newspapers throughout the Union. Prominent among those who urged the matter were Hon. John Bigelow, of New York, Colonel M. Richards Muckle, of Philadelphia, General Charles B. Norton, Professor John L. Campbell, now Secretary of the United States Centennial Commission, and others. Without attempting to detract from the merits of the numerous claimants who would wear the distinguished honor, yet it is but simple justice to the present age, and that history may be correct, to award the honor of the inception of the idea to Professor Campbell, who, in 1869, addressed the Hon. Morton McMichael, Mayor of Philadelphia, a letter setting forth the necessity and propriety of holding a National Exposition in Philadelphia during the year 1876. The letter was referred to Councils, but that body refused to take action on the suggestion, and the matter was permitted to drop for a time. Subsequently, the Franklin Institute, of Philadelphia, considered the matter in all its bearings, and finally addressed a communication to Councils, asking that a suitable tract in Fairmont Park should be set aside for the purposes of an Exhibition.

John L. Shoemaker, Esq., had the honor of presenting the communication to Council, and was thereupon made

Chairman of the Centennial Committee of that body, in which position he has up to the present time earnestly and faithfully labored for the advancement of the project. From the moment that the plan assumed a definite shape it has met with the warm encouragement of the people of the country, and its success is due in a great measure to this fact.

On February 24, 1870, both branches of Councils adopted a petition to Congress setting forth the importance of selecting Philadelphia as the place for holding an International Exhibition of arts and manufactures, and the products of the soil and mine, in 1876, in connection with the celebration of the Centennial Anniversary of American Independence. The matter was laid before Congress by Mayor Fox, heading a committee of Councils and a Legislative committee, and on the 9th of the following March, Hon. D. J. Morrell, chairman of the committee on Manufactures, introduced in the House of Representatives a bill providing for the holding of the Exhibition, which measure, after amendment and considerable delay, finally. on January 11, 1871, passed the House. In 1872 the bill became a law in consequence of passing the Senate and receiving the President's sanction. The Centennial Commission was formally organized on March 4, 1872, and the Board of Finance, May 10, 1873. On the 4th of July, 1874, Mayor Stokely removed the first shovel of earth from the spot on which now stands Memorial Hall, and the gigantic undertaking was then fairly and formally inaugurated, the completion of which was so auspiciously celebrated at the opening day.

THE EXHIBITION GROUNDS.

These are situated in the south-western extremity of Fairmount Park, bordering on the western shore of Schuylkill River. A reservation of 236 acres exclusively for exhibition purposes, was formally deeded to the Commission by the City of Philadelphia on July 4, 1873.

The buildings are located at a convenient distance from each other, and may be seen to great advantage from George's Hill, from the foot of which extends Machinery Hall, and beyond are the glass and iron walls of the Main Exhibition Building,—the two together forming an almost unbroken line of four thousand feet in length. The offices of the Commission and the Board of Finance lie a little south of Machinery Hall, near the railroad entrance, while directly north of them, beyond the line of the two great buildings, is the Judge's Hall for the use of the International Jury. The granite walls, with their iron dome surmounted by a colossal figure of Columbia, of the Memorial Hall, intended to be a National Art Gallery, are to be seen southward, and about midway of the Main Building. Still farther to the north, beyond a ravine shaded by lofty trees and spanned by a fine bridge, is the Horticultural Hall, overlooking the Schuylkill, while still farther north, and beyond a second ravine, is situated the building for Agriculture.

The garden of the Exhibition occupies the space between the Machinery Hall, the Horticultural, and the foot of George's Hill. In the arrangement of the grounds two leading features are noticeable. The first is Fountain Avenue, leading from Horticultural Hall to the foot of George's Hill, and crossed by a park drive, Belmont Avenue. The spaces formed by this intersection are divided as follows: The block bounded by Belmont Avenue, Fountain Avenue, and the Hill, is devoted to the British and other buildings for foreign commissioners, and the United States Government, and those for the different States. The block inclosed by Fountain Avenue and Machinery Hall has, as a distinctive feature, an artificial lake. On the north side of

Fountain Avenue, beyond the Park Drive, is the structure for the Women's Department, while east of Belmont Avenue, and south of Fountain, is the reservation for the buildings and garden of the Japanese Commission.

The statuary which has been erected by various societies includes the Colossal Fountain near the foot of George's Hill, which is 105 feet in diameter, and 35 feet in exterior height; the Columbus Monument, near the junction of Fountain and Belmont Avenues; the Humboldt Monument, the Hebrew statue of Religious Liberty, and the Witherspoon Monument. The fountain, which was erected by the Catholic Total Abstinence Society, at a cost of $50,000, is a centre from which radiate various avenues, chief of which are Fountain Avenue, and the Avenue of the Republic, which extends along the northern sides of the Machinery Hall and the Main Building. In addition to the avenues already mentioned, there is the Agricultural Avenue, State Avenue, Lansdowne Drive, and the drive to Belmont Mansion. Various walks leading through the grounds afford the visitor abundant opportunity to view their natural and artificial beauties, and give easy access to all parts of the inclosure. Among the principal entrances to the grounds may be mentioned the following :—

1st. East end of Main Building. The chief entrance for carriages.

2nd. Between the Main Building and Machinery Hall, for visitors coming by the Pennsylvania Railroad and the street cars.

3rd. Entrance from George's Hill.

4th. Entrance at the junction of Belmont Avenue and the Park Drive.

5th. Entrance for visitors by the Reading Railroad, at their depot.

6th. Entrance Belmont Valley for visitors by steam boats.

7th. Entrance in front of the Horticultural Hall.

8th. Entrance for visitors arriving on the Junction Railroad, and by steamboats in the Lansdowne Valley.

9th. Entrance to the Art Gallery. All of these entrances are fitted up with self-registering turnstiles.

In addition to being able to draw from the George's Hill City Reservoir, whose capacity is 40,000,000 gallons, the Exhibition will have an independent water supply from the Schuylkill River, where pumping engines capable of supplying 6,000,000 gallons daily have been placed.

THE EXHIBITION BUILDINGS.

The first conception of the number of buildings to be erected within the limits of the ground in Fairmont Park deeded to the Centennial authorities, pales into insignificance when one having thus conceived, now takes a position where a bird's eye view of the great enterprise can be obtained, and looks down upon the scene in all its vastness. As the eye wanders over acre upon acre of ground, upon which are erected edifices of every size, architectural style and beauty, the senses are bewildered, and it seems miraculous that such an undertaking should be so successfully consummated. The mind reverts to a time when this stretch of land upon which now everything is moving life, was merely a barren plateau awaiting the needs of the Fairmont Park Commission to be like the neighboring country, cultivated with shrubbery and laid out with walks and drives for the delectation of the people. In looking for a site upon which to construct the bufldings, this ground was found best adapted to the purposes, and it was selected.

The space covered by the buildings which have been erected reaches a total area of seventy-five acres, or twenty-five acres more than covered by buildings erected at any previous Exhibition, and the number of structures within the enclosure is 190. When one considers these facts, and consider what great labor has been performed in the raising of the funds, and the planning and construction of these buildings, all praise will certainly be extended to the men who have carried the burden of that labor upon their shoulders.

These one hundred and ninety buildings embrace the Exhibition Buildings proper, including the Main Building, Memorial Hall, Machinery Hall, Horticultural Hall, Agricultural Hall, the United States Government Building, and the Women's Pavillion, with their annexes, subsidiary Exhibition Buildings, buildings erected by foreign governments either as headquarters for their Commissioners or for exhibition purposes, buildings erected by States, to be used as headquarters for State Boards, State authorities, &c., buildings erected by States for exhibition purposes, buildings erected for the display of special industries, buildings erected by individual exhibitors for exhibition purposes, offices of the Centennial Commission and Board of Finance and buildings erected for the accommodation of the Centennial Guard and Centennial Fire Patrol ; buildings erected for purposes of traffic ; ornamental buildings, fountains, monuments, etc.; and minor structures.

THE MAIN BUILDING.

The Main Exhibition Building, the exponent perhaps of all the buildings within the Centennial enclosure, is a stupendeus work. Its great proportions make it a slight sublime, and belittles its sister edifice, which when considered for themselves cannot by any means be classed as finite. It covers an area of 21.47 acres, and consists of a parallelogram running east and west 1,880 feet, and 464 feet wide.

INTERNATIONAL EXHIBITION

PHILADELPHIA U. S. AMERICA

MAY 10TH NOVEMBER 10TH 1876.

MAIN EXHIBITION BUILDING.

1776 1876

Length,	-	-	-	-	-	-	-	1,876 feet.
Width,	-	-	-	-	-	-	-	464 "
Area,	-	-	-	-	-	-	nearly 21½ acres.

The larger portion of the structure is one-story in height, showing the main cornice on the outside at a distance of 45 feet from the ground, while the interior height is 70 feet.—

Upon the corners four towers arise to the height of 75 feet, and to secure architectural effect, the middle section of the roof, covering a space of 184 feet square, has been raised above the surrounding portion, and four towers, 48 feet square, rising to 120 feet in height, have been erected at the corners of this raised roof. The building is divided into a central avenue or nave, 120 feet in width; two avenues, each 100 feet in width; two aisles, each 48 feet wide; and two smaller aisles, each 24 feet wide.

The materials used in its construction are iron, glass, and wood, the total amount of iron used being 8,300,000 pounds. The exterior is finished with brick, wood in panels between the columns, and glazed sash; the corners and angles are accentuated by galvanized iron octagonal turrets, extending above the roof, surmounted with numerous flagstaffs and national eagle. The exterior is colored in yellow and brown tints, and in the interior the ceiling is painted very light blue. Grey picked with scarlet, black, and yellow, is the prevailing color for the upright iron columns and the trusses supporting the roof. It cost $1,600,000 to erect this structure, the work of which was began May 8, 1875, and the last girder placed in position November 18th, 1875.

The effort to obtain architectural effect has not been obtruded into the construction of the building, the design having been to obtain the best building possible for the particular purposes for which it was erected. Nevertheless the general appearance of the exterior is grand and imposing, and the interior has been richly decorated. The structure is lighted almost entirely from the side, and the greatest possible amount of light has been secured by constructing the sides of glass, and of as small columns as safety in construction would permit. This plan has resulted in the uniform distribution of light throughout the building, so that there

is no choice of location so far as light is concerned. This
is an admirable feature in an exhibition building, and one
which has never before been so fully and successfully introduced. The materials chiefly used in the construction are
glass and iron. Water, gas and drainage have been abun-
dantly supplied. Structures in the side aisles along the
sides of the building have been constructed for offices for
foreign commissioners in close proximity to the products exhibited. Offices for the officers of the Centennial Commission employed in administration have been placed at the end
of the building, and in the galleries on the sides. The division of the building into long avenues affords an equally fair
opportunity to exhibitors to display their goods to advantage.

The arrangement of the countries in sections includes
one prominent feature which is peculiar to this Exhibition,
and which is thoroughly international in conception. The
immense area of twenty-one acres covered by the building is
in the form of a parallelogram, divided by an avenue 30
feet wide running east and west through the centre, and
another avenue 30 feet wide running north and south
through the centre. This divides the floor space into four
central towers into each of the four grand sections. In order to embody the international feature with most effect the
leading nation of the four principal races of the world is
brought to the front of one of these four sections, thus :
France has the northeastern tower and adjacent space as
the representative of the Latin race; England has the north-
western tower and adjacent space as the reprepentative of
the Anglo-Saxon race ; Germany has the southwestern tower
and adjacent space as the representative of the Teutonic
races ; and the United States of America has the south-
eastern tower and adjacent space as the representative of the
combined Western races. These four great nations thus

14

come into competitive exhibition in the grand rectangular
space included between the four towers in the centre of the
building.

The system pursued in allotting space in the building
has been to cut the floor space into sections running north
and south, crosswise the building. These sections are divided by a grand central nave running east and west lengthwise
of the building. **The** floor space is thus broken **up into two
grand** divisions, that north of **the central nave and** that
south of it. North of the nave are the United States, **Mexico,** the Netherlands, Brazil, Belgium, **Switzerland, France**
and Colonies, Great Britain and Colonies, Sweden, **Norway**
and **Italy. South of the** nave are the United States (which
occupies space both north and south of the nave), Germany,
Austria and Hungary, Russia, Spain, **Turkey, Portugal,**
Egypt, Tunis, Sandwich Islands, Japan, China, Peru, Chili,
Argentine Republic, and Orange Free State of South Afri-
ca. It was originally contemplated to place the nations in
geographical order, **but this idea was** abandoned for several
reasons.

The following is the floor space occupied by the different nations :

The **United States** of America, in the Main Building,
196,881.1 square feet, and in the mineral annexe, 12,410
square feet, a total of 209,291 square feet. This space **is**
equal to nearly two-fifths of the total floor space in the building. Great Britain **and her colonies occupy** 99,917.9
square feet or nearly one-fifth **of the space** in the Main
Building proper **(not** including the mineral annexe). France
and colonies occupy 43,314.5 square **feet** or about one-
eleventh of the building. Germany has 27,705.5 square
feet or a little over one-twentieth. Austria and Hungary
occupy 24,070.8 square feet or about 3700 square feet less
than that occupied by Germeny. Sweden has 17,755.8

square feet or about .03 of the building. Belgium, 15,358.8 square feet, or about 2500 square feet less than Sweden; the Netherlands, 15,450 square feet, or a little more than Belguim ; Brazil, 6897 square feet, or a little over .01 of the building ; Japan has 17,080.8 square feet, or .03 of the total amount of floor space. Spain has 11,243 square feet, and Russia 11,002.8 square feet each being about .02 of the total space. The amount of floor space in square feet occupied by the other nations is as follows : Italy, 8167.5 ; Norway, 6897 ; Switzerland, 6646.8 ; Mexico, 6504.8 ; Chili and the Argentine Republic, 5647.5 ; Peru, 1462.5 ; Orange Free State, 1057.5 ; China, 5641 , Denmark, 2510 ; Turkey, 5022 ; Egypt, 5022 ; Tunis, 2016 ; Sandwich Islands, 1574.5, and Portugal, 3589.5.

MACHINERY HALL.

This structure is located about 550 feet west of the main Exhibition building ; and as its north front stands upon the same line, it is practically a continuation of that edifice, the two together presenting a frontage of 3824 feet from their eastern to their western ends upon the principal avenue within the grounds. This building consists of a main hall, 1402 feet long and 360 feet wide, with an annex on the southern side 208 feet by 210 feet. The entire area covered is 558,440 square feet, or nearly 13 acres, and the floor space afforded is about 14 acres. The chief portion of the building is one story in height, the main cornice upon the outside being 40 feet from the ground, and the interior height to the top of the ventilators in the avenues 70 feet, and in the isles 40 feet. To break the long lines of the exterior, projections have been introduced upon the four sides, and the main entrances are finished with facades extending to 78 feet in height. The eastern entrance will be the principal approach from railways, and from the main Exhibition building. Along the southern side are placed the boiler-houses, and such other buildings for special kinds of machinery as may be required. The plan of the Machinery build-

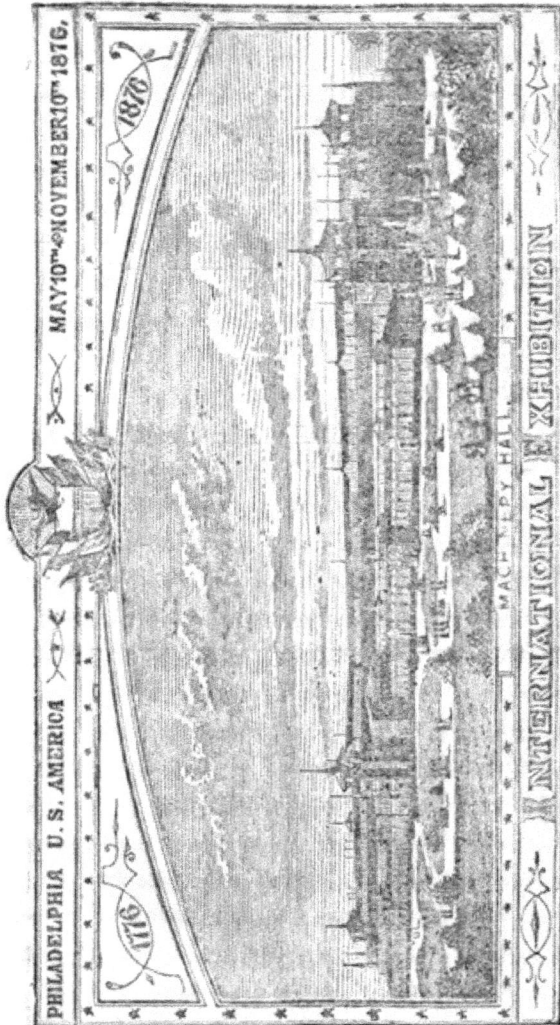

Length, — — — 3,824 feet.
Width, — — — 570 "
Area, — — — nearly 13 acres.

ing shows two main avenues 90 feet wide, with a central aisle between and an aisle on either side, these being 60 feet in width. These avenues and aisles together have 360 feet width, and each of them is 1360 feet long. At the centre of the building there is a transept of 90 feet width, which at the south end is prolonged beyond the building. This extend transept, beginning at 36 feet from the building and extending to 208 feet, is flanked on either side by aisles 60 feet wide, and forms an annex for hydraulic machines. The promenades are : in the avenue 15 feet wide, in the aisles 10 feet, and in the transept 25 feet. The walks extending across the building are all 10 feet wide, and lead at either end to exit doors. The foundations of this building are piers of masonry, the superstructure consisting of solid timber columns supporting roof-trusses constructed of straight wooden principal beams and wrought-iron ties and struts. The columns are placed in longitudinal lines, and in these rows stand 16 feet apart. The columns are 40 feet high, and support respectively the 90 feet roof-spans over the avenues at a height of 40 feet, and the 60 feet roof-spans over the aisles at the height of 20 feet. The outer walls are built of masonry to a height of 5 feet, and above that are composed of glazed sash between the columns. Portions of these sashes are movable for ventilation, and Louvre ventilators are introduced in continuous lengths over both the avenues and the aisles. The building is entirely lighted by side-light from the north and south.

Double lines of shafting are introduced into each avenue and aisle at a height about 20 feet. A Corliss steam-engine of 1400 horse-power drives the main shafting. There are also counter-lines of shafting in the aisles, and special steam-power furnished where necessary. Steam-power is furnished free to exhibitors. In the annex for hydraulic machine there is a tank 60 feet by 160 feet, with 10 feet depth of water. It is intended to exhibit all sorts of hydraulic machinery in full operation ; and at the southern end of the tank there is a waterfall 35 feet high by 40 feet wide, supplied from the tank by the pumps on exhibition.

THE ART GALLERY.

Three hundred feet north of the Main Building, on an elevated terrace, stands the Memorial Hall. The style of the building is the modern Renaissance. The materials used in its construction are granit, iron, and glass. It is thoroughly fire-proof, and will furnish a safe depository for the many works of art therein to be exhibited.

Its length is 365 feet, width 200 feet, and its height 59 feet.

From the central portion of the structure rises a dome of iron and glass to the height of 150 feet. Its bell shaped summit is surmounted by a colossal zinc statue of Columbia, 23½ feet high, weighing three tons. At each of the four corners of the base of the dome are groups representing Mining, Commerce, Agriculture, and Manufactures. Over the main entrance are two groups, representing Science and Art. Three distinctive features are displayed in the front of the building, namely : three large door-ways in the centre, a pavilion at each end, and arcades, similar in appearance to those in the old Roman villas, which connect the pavilions with the centre. The promenades thus formed look outward over the grounds and inward over open gardens ornamented with flowers, etc. The upper line of hese arcades forms a second promenade thirty-five feet above the ground. The walls of the east and west sides of the building are relieved by five niches for the reception of statues.

On the north front of the building arched windows take the place of the arcades. Between the pavilions, at an elevation of forty feet from the ground, extends a grand balcony 275 feet long and 45 feet width, from which a fine view is had of the park that stretches away to the northward.

The main door-ways give entrance to a reception hall appropriately frescoed and decorated. Its dimensions are

82 feet by 60, and the height to the ceiling 53 feet. From this hall, door-ways open directly into the central hall which is 83 feet square. The height of the ceiling of the dome which rises over it, is 80 feet. On either side of the central hall are galleries that form, with it, a grand hall nearly twice the size of any in the country, and large enough to contain 8,000 persons.

Beyond the side galleries are end galleries connecting with the pavilions at the corners of the building. The central hall and these galleries are lighted from above.

There are thirteen rooms on the north front of the building. Like the pavilions, they are lighted from the side. The pavilions and central hall are intended specially for the display of sculpture, and afford 11,921 square feet of floor surface. The various rooms and galleries for the exhibition of pictures present a total wall space of 71,992 square feet, and their capacity has been largely increased by the erection of temporary partitions in the galleries opening out of the centre hall.

The Art Gallery was erected by the State of Pennsylvania at a cost of $1,500,000. It is to remain after the close of the Exhibition, and serve the purpose of a National Memorial Hall, for the free exhibition of art treasures from all parts of the Union.

The contributions having been in excess of the space provided by Memorial Hall, an annex has been erected for the exhibition of paintings, which will be found directly north of the Art Gallery. The visitor will find an exit from the latter at the rear side, directly opposite the annex. Another annex will also be found between the main building and the gallery, at the right hand, or to the eastward, devoted exclusively to the display of photographic productions.

HORTICULTURAL HALL.

The city of Philadelphia made a liberal grant of money
to provide for the Horticultural department of the exhibi-

HORTICULTURAL HALL.

Length, - - - - - - - 383 feet.
Width, - - - - - - - 193 "

tion, an extremely ornate and commodious building, which is
designed to remain in permanence as an ornament of Fair-

mount Park. **This structure is** located on a terrace bordering the Schuylkill River, a short distance north of Memorial
Hall, and has a commanding view of the Schuylkill River
valley and the north-western portions of Philadelphia. **Ro-**
mantic ravines running down to the river are on **either side,**
separating it on the south from Memorial Hall and on the
north from Agricultural Building. These **ravines** are span-
ned by ornamental bridges **500** feet long **and 60** feet wide,
for convenience of access. Carriage-roads, **a** railway and
foot-walks pass **over** them. The Horticultural Building is
designed in the Moresque style of architecture of the twelfth
century, the chief materials externally being iron and glass,
supported by fine marble and brickwork. The building is
383 feet **long,** 193 feet wide **and** 72 feet high to the top of
the lantern. The main **floor is** occupied by the central conservatory, 230 feet **by 80 feet, and 55** feet high, surmounted
by a **lantern 170** feet long, 20 feet wide and 14 feet high.
Running entirely around this conservatory, at a height of 20
feet from the floor, is a gallery 5 feet wide. On the north
and south sides of **this principal room are** four forcing-houses
for **the** propagation **of young** plants, each of them 100 feet
by 30 feet, **and covered** by curved roofs of iron and glass,
which, **appearing upon the** exterior of the building, present
a **very fine feature. A vestibule** 30 feet square separates
the two forcing-houses on each side, and there are similar
vestibules at the centre of the east and west ends, on either
side **of** which **are** apartments for restaurants, reception-
rooms, offices, etc. Ornamental stairways lead from these
vestibules to the internal galleries of the conservatory, as
well as to four external galleries, each 100 feet long and 10
feet wide, which surmount the roofs of the forcing-houses.
These external galleries **are** connected with a grand promenade, formed by the roofs of the rooms **on** the lower floor,
giving a superficial area of about **17,000** square feet. The

east and west entrance to the Horticultural building are approached by flights of blue marble steps, from terraces 80 feet by 20 feet, in the centre of each of which stands an open kiosque 20 feet in diamater. Each entrance is beautified by ornamental tile and marble work, and the angles of the main conservatory are adorned with eight attractive fountains. The corridors connecting the conservatory with the surrounding apartments open fine vistas in every direction, and the beauties of the surrounding Park, and the river flowing in front and more than 100 feet beneath the building, add to the attractions. Extensive heating arrangements are provided in the basement, which is of fireproof construction, and the restaurant kitchens will also be located there.

Surrounding this building there are 35 acres of ground, which will be devoted to horticultural purposes, and are prepared for planting. In this plot there is an extensive series of sunken gardens.

THE AGRICULTURAL BUILDING.

This building, in which will be displayed all the products of the soil, both in the crude and manufactured condition, together with agricultural implements and machinery, is located east of Belmont Avenue, and to the north of Horticultural Hall. The structure, which is built of wood and glass, presents some novel features in its general plan and arrangement. The nave of the building, which is 800 feet in length, is intersected by a central and two side transepts, 540 feet long. These sections, in which the truss system is introduced, have the form of a Gothic arch springing from the ground, to an altitude of 75 feet, the intervening spaces between them being inclosed and covered by ornamental roofs. The entire area within the building, for exhibition purposes, is nine and one half acres. The peculiar form of the roof section is calculated to decrease the intensity of the sun's rays, to which, if unprotected by any ceiling beneath, it would be subjected in the summer season. The building is remarkable for economy of space and simplicity of construction rather than embellishment.

INTERNATIONAL EXHIBITION

MAY 10ᵗʰ ⚬ NOVEMBER 10ᵗʰ 1876.

1876

1776

PHILADELPHIA U. S. AMERICA

AGRICULTURAL HALL.

Length,		540 feet.
Width,		820 "
Area,		10¼ acres.

In the ground plan, four avenues divide the building into sections, each of which has aisles 13 feet wide by 197 feet long extending through it to the north and south avenue at one end and into the side passages at the other. Three of the main avenues run east and west through the building, one through the centre being 540 feet long by 60 feet wide, the other two are the same length and 30 feet in width. The fourth main avenue extends through the middle of the structure and is 826 feet long by 70 wide.

The Stock-yard, twenty-two acres in extent, is situated five hundred yards from the principal entrance to the Agricultural Building, outside of the Centennial inclosure. The display of Live Stock will take place during the months of September and October, the periods assigned to each class and family being as follows :—

Horses, mules, and asses,	from Sept. 1 to Sept. 15.		
Horned cattle,	" Sept. 20 " Oct. 5.		
Sheep, swine, goats, and dogs,	" Oct. 10 " Oct. 25.		
Poultry,	" Oct. 25, " Nov. 10.		

A trial of Harvesting Machinery will be given during June and July ; and after the removal of the crops, Tillage Implements will be tested on the same grounds.

THE UNITED STATES EXHIBITS BUILDING.

The Exhibits of the General Government will be presented in a building situated on Belmont Avenue, north of Fountain Avenue. Its cost was about $60,000. It has a floor area of 82,640 square feet, a length of central nave and aisles of 400 feet, by 100 feet in width, and a transept 300 feet long by 100 feet wide. The building is constructed entirely of wood. About $500,000 has been appropriated by the government for its exhibition purposes, and the various Departments and the Smithsonian Institution will be fully represented.

The purpose of this exhibition is to "illustrate the functions and administrative faculties of the government in time of peace, and its resources as a new power, and thereby serve to demonstrate the nature of our institutions and their adap. tation to the wants of the people." To give effect to the purpose of the government, a Board has been created of seven members, one each from the War, Treasury, Navy, Interior, Post Office, and Agricultural Departments, and the Smith sonian Institution to which is intrusted the care of the entire Exhibit.

ARRIVING AT PHILADELPHIA.

Canadian visitors to the Centennial will mostly arrive at Philadelphia by either the Pennsylvania, or the Phila- delphia and Reading Railways. By perusing the different routes presented in this volume, it will be seen that each line touching the Canadian border, connects with each of these lines of Railways, which cross each other at German- town Junction, a few miles out of the city. Passengers taking the Pennsylvania Road at any point between Jersey City and Philadelphia can land directly at the Centennial buildings and opposite the entrance to the grounds between the Main building and Machinery Hall, or can go down town to the Depot proper between 32nd and 33rd streets as heretofore described.

Those connecting with the Philadelphia and Reading Road at Allentown or Bethlehem, can get off at a depot near the eastern end of the Main building or go into the city to the Depot at the corner of Callowhill and Broad or 13th streets, sixteen blocks farther down town than if the arrival had been on the Pennsylvania Road. But in no case would we recommend visitors, who have travelled such a distance as Canadians must, to stop off at the grounds, unless boarding accommodations are previously secured in that quarter. It is much more satisfactory to go direct to the hotel or board- ing house, and after resting and securing such information as cannot be obtained in a work so limited as the Guide, take the street cars to the grounds.

MEMORIAL HALL.

THE CITY OF PHILADELPHIA.

Philadelphia is one of the best laid out cities on the continent, and after a stranger once understands the method of naming and numbering its streets, it is an easy matter to find any locality which it may be desirable to visit. In order to be found *au fait* to the task at all times, it is quite necessary that the points of the compass should be perfectly understood the first time the stranger arrives there, as it is ever afterwards a difficult matter to locate points of interest, when the visitor gets "turned around," to use the common phraseology, or when one gets north, south, east and west, somewhat mixed. To prevent such occurences, and give a detailed description, we may be pardoned for addressing the reader in the first person :—

Supposing you arrive at the city depot of the Pensyl‑vania Railway. On passing from the depot you observe a street running to the right and left, parrellel with the front of the building. This, is Market Street, the dividing line of the city. If you take one of the Market street cars going to the right you will go direct west, and will find the terminus in the country. If you choose the same line of cars going in the opposite direction, you will go eastward, and remaining in it until you reach the eastern terminus, you will be landed at the bank of the Delaware River, the eastern boundary of the city, across which can be seen the city of Camden in New Jersey. Learning this, it is an easy matter to recollect that Market street and all other parellel streets run east and west, the city proper being eastward.

The city being divided by Market street, all that portion to the right as you go eastward, is south, or as it is called, " below," and that to the left, north, or " above."

Facing the east, the first street to the right parellel with Market, is Chestnut, the Broadway of Philadelphia, then comes Walnut, followed by Locust, Spruce, Pine, Lombard,

South, Bainbridge, etc., etc. The first to the left is Arch, the next Race, followed by Vine, Callowhill, Spring Garden, Green, Wallace, etc., etc.

The cross streets run parellel, and being at right angles to Market, of course run north and south, those to the right going south, and those to the left leading northwards. These are not named, but numbered, commencing at the Delaware River with *first*, and ending with *sixtieth*, 30 blocks west of the depot, which is between 32nd and 33rd.

We will now suppose you have rooms engaged at the Merchants Hotel on " 4th street, below Market." You select a Market street car, going " down." Four or five rods below, you pass 32nd st., over which you would pass if you took the Chestnut street cars in front of the depot, and after passing 31st and 30th, you reach a bridge over the Schuylkill, (' School-Kill') the stream which seperates West Philadelphia, from the eastern or principal business portion. On arriving at 4th st., you leave the car and go south until you reach the hotel. You may understand that it is between Market and Chestnut, for, if it had been beyond the latter, your hotel card would have read, " below Chestnut," instead of " below Market."

Another point peculiar to Philadelphia streets, is in the numbering. Every block contains exactly 100 numbers, the odd numbers appearing on one side of a street and the even figures on the other. The numbering on the north and south, or cross streets commence at Market, on either side.

To show how easily one can find any location when the numbering is once understood, we will give one or two selections, knowing from personal experience the value of such knowledge when once attained. 637 north 15th st., is the point you wish to reach, from the corner of Market and 4th sts. That would be 11 streets west and 6 blocks north. You take a car for 15th street, get out there and take a 15th street car, on the north side of Market. On looking at the numbers on the right hand you find No. 7, which indicates that the number you are in search of, is on the opposite side, as it is an even number. Again, supposing you are located at the corner of Walnut and 23rd street, and wish to go to 213 north 10th st. As Walnut is south of Market, the latter must be crossed to the north side. 213 north 10th street will then be easily found by proceeding to 10th st., and going above, two blocks and thirteen doors on the side of the odd numbers.

3254 Chestnut could be found between 32nd and 33rd streets, on Chestnut, there being also 100 numbers between each cross street from the first to the sixteeth, or last street.

Taking Market Street as a center of calculation, and remembering that a block always contains but 100 numbers, it will be found an easy matter to locate most any place in the city.

STREET RAILWAYS.

No city in the United States possesses as great a number of street railways which charge as reasonable rates, as Philadelphia. The cars are much superior in neatness and comfort to those of New York. The fare on any line is 7 cents for each trip, but the passenger can, and should purchase of the conductor, 25 or 50 cents worth of tickets, which are good on any road in the city. Four tickets will be given for 25 cents. If the passenger is on or near the line on which he is travelling, a single fare is sufficient, but if he has to go some distance on a cross street he hands the conductor 9 cents and asks for an exchange. This exchange or extra ticket will carry you over the connecting lines, and saves five cents to the one who understands the "dodge" which is not usually made known to strangers. "The Union Line" runs principally on the cross streets running north and south and does not exchange with other lines. When an exchange is required, it is advisable to ask the conductor if he exchanges with cars on the street with which the connection is to be made.

Another point in connection with the street railways, which visitors should bear in mind, is the difference in running the cars, to what is exhibited in other cities. With the exception of Market, nearly all the principal Streets of the city are narrow, and do not admit of two tracks or of running the cars in but one direction. In Market street there are two tracks, but in the parallel streets only one is allowed. In Chestnut street, the cars all move eastward ; in Walnut they run westward ; in Locust eastward and so on throughout the city.

HOW TO REACH THE GROUNDS.

The Exhibition Grounds can be reached in three ways ; by street railway, railroad, or by steamer. Nearly all the street cars running east and west, either run direct to the Grounds or connect with those that do, so that it is an easy matter, to find a car going in that direction.— Owing to the usually crowded condition of street cars at present, especially after they pass 8th or 9th streets, it is much preferable to go to the depot of the Philadelphia and Reading Road at Callowhill street, and take the passenger cars of that most excellent road. The fare is only ten cents and a payment of 15 cents on the 13th or 15th street cars will procure a ticket over both roads, to the depot near the grounds. The Reading Road passes through a portion of Fairmount Park, and affords a faint glimpse of the beauties afforded by that charming retreat, the largest Park on the continent of America. Passengers going to the Exhibition grounds by this railroad, which is considered the quickest route, will enter the grounds at the east end of the Main building, or the turn-stiles adjoining on the north side.

If the visitor is located some distance above 15th street, it would be advisable to take a car direct to the grounds. If the trip is made by a Walnut, Chestnut or Market street car, the approach to the Exhibition will be by Lancaster Avenue, from the Pennsylvania Railroad depot to 44th street, and from thence by Belmont Avenue. Those going by the north side routes, generally approach the grounds by Elm Avenue, parallel with the line of the Main and Machinery buildings. Visitors will find more trouble in getting a seat in returning to the city at night, than on leaving it earlier in the day. To prevent this annoyance as much as possible, we would advise those returning to the city by Belmont Avenue, to walk down that street on the left hand side, as far as the depot of that line (about twenty or thirty rods,) and take a seat in a car that will soon start for the triangular space in front of the Exhibition buildings, and return to the city as soon as loaded. This plan is adopted by citizens and will insure a good seat without extra expense, something very acceptable after an all day tramp inside the grounds.

Another method of reaching the grounds, is by street Railway to the landing of the Fairmount steamers on the Schuylkill, which can be reached by cars running westward on the north side of Market or by any of the cross streets below 24th. The landing is at the lower end of Fairmount Park on the east side, about six blocks above the Market street Bridge. This way of going to or coming from the grounds, will prove the most pleasant of the three, and should not be neglected. Taking the steamer at the landing opposite Green street, you pass Lemon Hill on the right, on which stands the Mansion of Robt. Morris of revolutionary fame, and to the front of it on the river margin, are the

elegant boat houses of the Schuylkill Navy. On the left
side will be noticed the Zoological Gardens occupying 35
acres. As you ascend the river you find a number of invit-
ing summer houses for the use of pedestrains, and a little
north, "Grants Cottage" a small cabin which was used by
General Grant as his headquarters at City Point, Virginia,
during the last year of the war. Nearer the bridge is the
Guard House for lost children, a building that is frequently
in use during the summer months. Passing on up the river,
the eye is delighted with the natural beauty witnessed on
both sides of a very dirty stream until the Centennial landing is reached on the left, from which you ascend through a
romantic ravine to the eastern end of the Main building.

INSIDE THE ENCLOSURE.

The favorite entrance to the Exhibition grounds is on
Elm Avenue opposite Belmont Avenue, between the Main
building and Machinery Hall. Before attempting to enter
the grounds, furnish yourself with a fifty cent scrip. If you
have none, step into the Centennial Bank at the right hand
and get a bill changed. Passing through the turn stile you
are confronted with a large square between the two buildings mentioned, in the centre of which is the Bartholdi
Fountain, made by Major Auguste Bartholdi of Paris, and
presented to the Commissioners of Fairmount Park. After
making an inspection of this justly celebrated work of art,
we would advise a trip around the grounds on the miniature
railway, before entering any of the buildings, for two reasons.
First, the visitor is somewhat fatigued before reaching the Exhibition, and second, a tour of the grounds
gives one a better understanding of the various localities to
be visited, which will afterwards be of much value, besides
affording a temporary respite from the sometimes arduous
task of riding four or five miles in a crowded street car.

Turning to the right, and crossing the square, diagonally, to the corner of the main building, you strike the Avenue of the Republic, running parallel with the buildings, and take a car at **the first** station, a building about the size of a soda fountain but not so large as some of those which will be seen before leaving the main structure. Passing the junction of Belmont Avenue, the first building of a foreign style is the office of Cook & Sons, the great English Railway Ticket Agents for tourists' routes. Immediately beyond **is** a miniature lake, from the surface of which **rises several** hundred streams, in **a** circle, making an appearance wonderfully attractive. Arriving at the western end of Machinery Hall, the course is obstructed by a fountain erected by the Catholic Total Abstinence Society at an expense of $30,000. **The** track **here turns** to the left, crossing a plateau behind **the** Hall, and **makes a circle around** to **the west side of the fountain,** passing **by several** buildings for the display of **special** articles of manufacture, **the** largest **of which is a saw mill.** Opposite the fountain, at **the** left, **is the** Missouri State building ; **next,** a little farther back, **Arkansas,** after **which comes the buildings of the English** Government, **the** most extensive on **the grounds, and easily** recognized **by the** quaintness **of** the **architecture and leaden** window **sash.** Beyond **the** English, **on the same** side, **is the New York** State building, followed in rotation **by** that of Massachusetts, Connecticut, New Hampshire, **Mi**chigan, Wisconsin, (where can be seen **the famous** eagle, " Old **Abe,"** which accompanied **a** Wisconsin regiment **through the** whole war) Illinois, Indiana and Ohio. Opposite these state buildings **are those of** the Government **of the** United **States.**

After crossing Belmont Avenue, **the** track passes around the green-roofed Agricultural Hall, behind which, **on** the right, will be **seen** the Annex, Wagon, Brewers', and **Pomological** Buildings. After passing the latter, on the left will be seen the Model Butter and Cheese **Factory,** followed by the Tea and Coffee Exhibition Building. The train now passes between the Agricultural **Hall** and Lauber's American **restaurant,** the proprietor of which **pays** $80,000 for **the** privilege of feeding the hungry, and quenching the thirsty with lager **beer** at **five** cents a glass. Returning to Belmont Avenne again, on the left·hand corner another restaurant will be found, called "The South." From this point the track follows Belmont Avenue until it reaches the station at the starting point, **and** passes successively the Kansas State building, **Womens** School **House,** Womans Pavillion, Egyptian Mosque and numerous others. A Drinking Pavillion will be passed at Fountain Avenue and Belmont **and by looking up the former street to the** left will be seen the beautiful Horticultaral **Hall.**

CENTENNIAL ROUTES.

In this Department of the Guide, will **be found a list of** the various Routes from the Canadian Frontier, to Philadelphia and return, **and** the latest schedule **of** rates. It **will** be noticed **that some of them** afford an opportunity **of** visiting various Summer **Resorts, either going or** returning, at **excursion** rates. None **of them** afford **more** pleasant or **varied** routes than **the Rome,** Watertown & Ogdensburg and the Utica and Black **River** Railways, **both** of which are accessible **from** Ottawa, **Prescott,** Perth, Smith Falls, Cornwall, Brockville, Gananoque, **Kingston,** Napanee and **Belleville.**

ROME, WATERTOWN & OGDENSBURG ROAD.

Good For Thirty Days.

Route No. 1.—Ferry from Prescott to R., W. & O. wharf, Ogdensburg; Ogdensburg to Rome by Rome & Watertown Road; New York Central to New York.

Arriving at the 42nd Street depot, take a 4th Avenue car, which will be found in the depot, and go to Grand or Courtland street, and thence to Pennsylvania ferry. Fare 6 cents on each road. If you wish to use the coupon, take a Transfer coach at the depot, which will also land you at the ferry.

Arriving at Jersey City, follow the crowd straight ahead to the reception room ; get your tickets out, present them to the gate-keeper at the farther end, for inspection, pass through and take the left hand train. If the Central Road is on time, and it has an envied reputation for that feature of its management, you will reach Jersey City in time to take the 8:35 a. m. train (providing you leave Ogdensburg at 2:45 p. m., or Cape Vincent at 4:40 p. m.,) and arrive at Philadelphia at 12:05 noon. But if you wish to loiter at New York or Jersey City until 9:25 a. m., you can have the choice of two trains leaving at the same time, one of which will land you at Philadelphia at 12:45 noon, and the other at 12:10, only five minutes later than the one leaving at 8:35. This fast train is called the " Limited," and is a special favorite with the travelling public, from the fact of its being composed wholly of Pullman Drawing Room cars, making the trip of 90 miles in two hours and thirty-five minutes, with only two stops, at Newark and Trenton. If you wish to enjoy the *creme de la creme* of railroad arrangements, by all means avail yourself of an opportunity of a trip by it, either going or coming. The extra fare is only $1, each passenger. The railroad fare from Ogdensburg to Philadelphia and return by the same route, or by the "Day" or "Peoples'" line of steamers, from New York to Albany, at the option of the purchaser, $20.55. From Cape Vincent, $18.45. Trains leaving Ogdensburg at 7:30 a. m., or Cape Vincent at 8 a. m., reach New York at 10 p. m., Philadelphia at 4:30 a. m. next day. Passengers leaving at this hour must lie over at Jersey City until 12 o'clock midnight, but if they choose, can take a sleeping car at that station as soon as they arrive there. This car arrives at Philadelphia at 4:30 next morning, but the passengers have the privilege of remaining in their berths until 8 o'clock if they choose, a feature that is of much service to travellers arriving at

New York or Jersey City by the way of the New York Central or Erie Railways. The charge for a berth is $1.50. All tickets over the Central Road, between Albany and New York, are good on People's Line, or Day Line of steamers, either up or down the Hudson.

The above answers for all connections with the New York Central Road. We might also add : nearly every train on the Pennsylvania Road, has Palace cars, in which the charge for a seat is 50 cents.

Route No. 2.—Rome Watertown & Ogdensburg R. R. to Syracuse ; Delaware, Lackawanna & Western to Manunka Chunk ; Pennsylvania R. R. to Philadelphia. Returning by same route.
Fare from Cape Vincent...... ....$16.45
Fare from Ogdensburg........................... 18.55
This route passes through Chenango Falls ; Binghampton, the seat of the Inebriate Asylum, and a prominent Summer Resort ; Scranton ; and Trenton, New Jersey.

Route No. 3.—Rome, Watertown & Ogdensburg R. R. to Sterling Junction ; Southern Central R. R. to State Line ; Lehigh Valley R. R. to Allentown or Bethlehem ; Philadelphia and Reading R. R. or North Pennsylvania R. R. to Philadelphia. Returning by same route.
Fare from Cape Vincent.............. ....$16.45
Fare from Ogdensburg...................... ..... 18.55
This route passes through Oswego, Auburn, Wilkesbarre and Mauch Chunk, Pa. Passengers on arriving at Allentown, about 50 miles from Philadelphia, have a choice of two roads. If they choose the North Pennsylvania their Philadelphia terminus will be at American and Burk streets, 19 blocks North of Market, between 2nd and 3rd. Street cars run South on 2nd Street.

Route No. 4.—Rome, Watertown and Ogdensburg R. R. to Sterling Junction ; Southern Central R. R. to Allentown or Bethlehem , Philadelphia & Reading R. R. or North Pennsylvania R. R. to Philadelphia ; Pennsyvlania

R. R. to New York ; New York Central & Hudson River
R. R. to Rome ; Rome, Watertown & Ogdensburg R. R.
to Starting Point.

Fare from Cape Vincent.. .. ..$17.45
Fare from Ogdensburg.................... ... . 19.55

Route No. 5.—Rome, Watertown & Ogdensburg R. R.
to Syracuse ; Delaware, Lackawanna & Western R. R. to
Manunka Chunk ; Pennsylvania R. R. to Philadelphia.
Returning, Pennsylvania R. R. to New York ; New York
Central & Hudson River R. R. to Rome ; Rome, Water-
town & Ogdensburg R. R. to Starting Point.

Fare from Cape Vincent................. ......:....$17.45
Fare from Ogdensburg........................... 19.55

Route No. 6.—Rome, Watertown & Ogdensburg R. R.
to Oswego ; Delaware, Lackawanna & Western to Manunka
Chunk ; Pennsylvania R. R. to Philadelphia, and return
by same route.

Fare from Cape Vincent.............................$16.45
Fare from Ogdensburg...... .... 18.55

Route No. 7.—Rome, Watertown & Ogdensburg R.R.
to Oswego ; Delaware, Lackawanna & Western to Manunka
Chunk ; Pennsylvania R. R. to Philadelphia. Pennsyl-
vania R. R. to New York ; New York Central & Hudson
River R. R. to Rome ; Rome Watertown & Ogdensburg R.
R. to Starting Point.

Fare from Cape Vincent............... .... $17:45
Fare from Ogdensburg. 19.55

Route No. 8.—Rome, Watertown & Ogdensburg R. R.
to Syracuse ; Delaware, Lackawanna & Western R. R. to
Manunka Chunk ; Pennsylvania R. R. to Philadelphia ;
North Pennsylvania R. R. or Philadelphia & Reading R.
R. to Bethlehem or Allentown ; Lehigh Valley R. R. to
Waverly ; Erie R. R. to Elmira ; Northern Central R. R.
to Watkins ; Seneca Lake Steamers to Geneva ; New York
Central and Hudson River R. R. to Syracuse ; Rome,
Watertown & Ogdensburg R. R. to Starting Point.

Fare from Cape Vincent. $17.45
Fare from Ogdensburg................................. 19.55

This is a very desirable route, as it affords a visit to Watkins Glen, the famous Summer Resort which is little inferior in popularity to Niagara Falls, and also confers on the tourist the pleasure of a ride over Seneca Lake, 40 miles in length, and one of the prettiest bodies of water on the Continent.

Route No. 9.—Rome, Watertown & Ogdensburg R. R. to Syracue ; **New York** Central & Hudson River R. R. to Geneva ; **Seneca** Lake Steamers to Watkins ; Northern Central R. R. to Elmira ; Erie R. R. to Waverly ; Lehigh Valley R. R. to Allentown or Bethlehem ; Philadelphia & Reading R. R. or North Pennsylvania R. R. to Philadelphia , Pennsylvania R. R. to New York ! New York Centrrl & Hudson River R. R. to Rome ; Rome, Watertown & Ogdensburg R. R. to Starting Point.

Fare same as No. 8.

Route No. 10.—Rome, Watertown & Ogdensburg R. R. to Syracuse ; Delaware, Lackawanna & Western R. R., to Manunka Chunk ; Pennsylvania R. R. to Philadelphia ; Pennsylvania R. R. to New York ; Erie R. R. to Binghamton ; Delaware, Lackawanna & Western R. R. to Syracuse ; **Rome,** Watertown & Ogdensburg R. R. to Starting Point.

Fare same as No. 8.

Route No. 11.—Rome, Watertown & Ogdensburg R.R. to Syracuse ; Delaware, Lackawanna & Western R. R. to Binghampton ; Erie R. R. to New York ; Pennsylvania R. R. to Philadelphia, returning by same route.

Fare from Cape Vincent.............................$18.45
from Ogdensburg................................. 20.55

By this route passengers arrive in Jersey City on **the** Erie Railway, and are taken to the Depot of the Pennsylvania Road by street cars running between the depots of the two lines. Passengers by the Erie will find the scenery. **the more pleasant going East, on** the left side of the car.

Route No. 12.—Rome, Watertown & Ogdensburg R. R. to Syracuse ; Delaware, Lackawanna & Western R. R. to Binghamton ; Erie R. R. to New York ; Pennsylvania, R. R. to Philadelphia. Returning—Pennsylvania R. R. to Manunka Chunk, Delaware, Lackawanna & Western R. R. to Syracuse ; Rome, Watertown & Ogdensburg R. R. to Starting Point.

Fare from Cape Vincent.............................$17.45
From Ogdensburg................................... 19.55

Route No. 13.—Rome, Watertown & Ogdensburg R. R. to Rome ; New York Central & Hudson River R. R. to New York; Pennsylvania R. R. to Philadelphia. Returning—North Pennsylvania R. R. or Philadelphia & Reading R. R. to Bethlethem or Allentown ; Lehigh Valley R. R. to Waverly ; Erie R. R. to Elmira ; Northern Central R. R. to Watkins ; Seneca Lake Steamers to Geneva ; New York Central & Hudson River R. R. to Syracuse ; Rome, Watertown & Ogdensburg R. R. to starting point.

Fare same as No. 12.

By this route passengers can have the advantages in scenic views, mentioned farther on in the New York Central list, and also the beauties of Seneca Lake and Watkin's Glen.

Route No. 16.—Rome, Watertown & Ogdensburg R. R. to Syracuse ; Delaware, Lackawanna & Western R. R. to Manunka Chunk ; Pennsylvania R. R. to Philadelphia ; Pennsylvania R. R. to Harrisburg ; Northern Central R. R. to Sunbury ; Pennsylvania R. R. (P. & E. Div) to Williamsport ; Northern Central R. R. to Watkins ; Seneca Lake Steamers to Geneva ; New York Central & Hudson River R. R. to Syracuse ; Rome, Watertown & Ogdensburg R. R. to Starting Point.

From Cape Vincent..........................$17.45
From Ogdensburg............................ 19.55

Route No. 17.—Rome, Watertown & Ogdensburg R. R. to Syracuse ; New York Central & Hudson River R. R. to Geneva ; Seneca Lake Steamers to Watkins ; Northern Central R. R. to Williamsport ; Pennsylvania R. R. (P. &

E. Div) to Sunbury; Northern Central R. R. to Harrisburg, Pennsylvania R. R. to Philadelphia; Pennsyluania R. R. to New York; New York Central R. R. to Rome; Rome, Watertown & Ogdensburg R. R. to Starting Point.

From Ogdensburg.... ....$19.55
From Cape Vincent.... .... 17.45

Route No. 18.—Rome, Watertown & Ogdensburg R. R. to Syracuse; New York Central & H. R. R. R. to New York; Pennsylvannia R. R. to Philadelphia; Pennsylvania R. R. to Harrisburg; Northern Central R. R. to Sunbury; Pennsylvania R. R. (P. & E. Div) to Williamsport; Northern Central R. R. to Watkins; Seneca Lake Steamers to Geneva; New York Central & Hudson River R. R. to Syracuse; Rome, Watertown & Ogdensburg R. R. to Starting Point.

From Ogdensburg........................... . ...$19.55
From Cape Vincent........................ .... 17.45

UTICA & BLACK RIVER RAILWAY.

In the following list of Routes by this Road, passengers have Centennial reduced rates from Route No. 1 to No. 6. From No. 7 to No. 14 they have the benefit of Centennial rates to Philadelphia, and Summer excursion rates to all other points on the return trip. The remarks applying to the Rome & Watertown, apply to a majority of the Routes of this Road. The tickets are all good from Brockville to Morristown by Ferry, and include a return trip to starting point. Fare payable in American funds. Tickets good for 30 days.

Route No. 1.—Ferry to Morristown; U. & B. R. R. to Utica; N. Y. C. & H. R. R. R. to New York; Jersey City Ferry to Jersey City; Penn. R. R. to Philadelphia. Returning by same route.

Fare from Brockville........... ....$19.95

Route No. 2.—Ferry to Morristown; U. & B. R. R. R. to Utica; D., L. & W. R. R. to Manunka Chunk; Penn. R. R. to Philadelphia. Returning by same route.

Fare from Brockville............. .... $18.60

Route No 3.—Ferry to Morristown ; U. & B. R. R. R. to Utica , N. Y. C. & H. R. R. to New York ; Jersey City Ferry to Jersey City ; Penn. R. R. to Philadelphia ; Penn. R. R. to Manunka Chunk ; D., L. & W. R. R. to Utica ; Utica to Brockville.

Fare from Brockville..... ....$19.60

Route No. 4.—Ferry to Morristown; U. & B. R. R. R. to Utica ; D., L. & W. R. R. to Binghamton ; Erie R. R. to New York ; Jersey City Ferry to Jersey City ; Penn. R. R. to Philadelphia ; Penn. R. R. to Manunka Chunk ; D., L. & W. R. R. to Utica ; U. & B. R. R. R. and Ferry to Brockville.

Fare from Brockville...................... ....$19.60

Route No. 5.—Ferry to Morristown; U. & B. R. R. R. to Utica ; D., L. & W. R. R. to Manunka Chunk ; Penn. R. R. to Philadelphia ; Penn. R. R. to New York ; Pavonia Ferry to New Jersey ; Erie R. R. to Binghamton : D., L. & W. R. R. to Utica ; U. & B. R. R. R. and Ferry to Brockville.

Fare from Brockville $19.60

Route No. 6.—Ferry to Morristown; U. & B. R. R. R. to Utica ; D., L & W. R. R. to Binghamton ; Erie R. R. to New York ; Jersey City Ferry to Jersey City ; Penn. R. R. to Philadelphia ; Penn. R. R. to New York ; Pavonia Ferry to Jersey City ; Erie R. R. to Binghamton ; D., L. & W. R. R. to Utica ; U. & B. R. R. R. and Ferry to Brockville.

Fare from Brockville............................. .... $19.95

Route No. 7.—U. & B. R. R. R. to Utica ; N. Y. C. & H. R. R. R. to New York; Jersey City Ferry to Jersey City : Pennsylvania R. R to Philadelphia ; Pennsylvania R. R. to Harrisburg ; N. C. R. R. to Sunbury ; Pennysl-vania (P. & E. Div.) to Williamsport; N. C. R. R. to Canandaigua ; N. Y. C. & H. R. R. R. to Niagara Falls ; N.Y. C. & H. R. R. R. to Utica; U. & B. R. R. R. & Ferry to Brockville.

Rate..$27.50

This route is an excellent one for varied scenery, and

passes over the most interesting portion of Pennsylvania. The return route passes through Lancaster, Pa., Elmira, Watkins, Rochester, Syracuse and Rome, N. Y., and affords an opportunity of visiting the greatest summer resort of the world, Niagara Falls.

Arriving at Niagara Falls, omnibusses will be found at the depot, of the Spencer, Cataract, International, Park Place, Niagara, and Falls Hotel, on the American side, and Clifton House, and Prospect House on the Canadian side. With the exception of those on the Canada side, it is a very short walk to any of the Houses mentioned.

The fare at the hotels are as follows : Spencer, $3.50 ; Park Place, $3 ; International, $4.50; Cataract, $4.50 ; Falls, $2.50; and Niagara, $2.50 per day. The Falls Hotel, Spencer House, and Niagara House, run free omnibuses. The Clifton House and Prospect House rates are, respectively, $3 and $2.50 per day in gold. The Clifton House is at the end of the new Suspension Bridge, and the Falls Hotel, near the Canadian Falls. Both are well kept, and afford a full view of the whole Falls from the veranda.

Hack hire is $2 an hour, or so much for the whole trip. In engaging one, have it understood what points should be visited before starting. If the tourist has a day to spare, it is much cheaper and pleasanter to go on foot. By this method the whole expense for one person will be only $1.25.

In visiting Goat Island, take the forenoon. On reaching the Island, the overseer's house will be seen in front, at which point a path turns to the right, one to the left, and one goes straight ahead. Although the programme handed you at the toll gate advises turning to the right, yet we think it advisable to follow the straight path past the overseer's house, and take the first branch to the left, which leads to the Sister Islands. After viewing these, go around the island to the right, to the starting point. Visit the

Canada side in the afternoon, for the best rainbow effect, going across the river by the bridge, and returning by the Ferry, into **Prospect Park.**

Route No 8.—U. & B. R. R. R. to Utica; N. Y. C. & H. R. R. R. to Niagara Falls ; N. Y. C. H. & H. R. R. R. to Canandaigua ; N.C.R.R. to Williamsport ; Pennsylvania (P. & E. Div.) to Sunbury; N. C. R. R. to Harrisburg ; Pennsylvania R. R. to Philadelphia ; Pennsylvania R. R. to New York ; Peoples' Line Steamers to Albany ; N. Y. C. & H. R. R. R. to Utica ; U. & B. R. R. R. to Brockville. Rate..$27.95

Route No. 9.—U. & B. R. R. R. to Utica ; N. Y. C. & H. R. R. R. to New York ; Jersey City Ferry to Jersey City ; Pennsylvania R. R. to Philadelphia ; P. W. & B. R. R. to Baltimore ; B. & P. R. R. to Washington ; B. & P. R. R. to Baltimore ; N. C. R. R. to Sunbury ; Pennsylvania (R. & E. Div.) to Williamsport ; N. C. R. R. to Canandaigua ; N. Y. C. & H. R. R. R. to Niagara Falls; N. Y. C. & H. R. R. R. to Utica ; U. & B. R. R. R. & Ferry to Brockville. Rate...$32.25

It would be hard to conceive of a route giving as much travel for so little money, as the above, especially when the holder of a ticket can stop off at any place he may choose.

Route No. 10.—U. & B. R. R. R. to Utica ; N. Y. C. & H. R. R. R. to New York ; Jersey City Ferry to Jersey City ; Pennsylvania R. R. to Philadelphia ; P. & R. or N. N. P. R. R. to Allentown or Bethlehem ; L. V. R. R. to Waverly ; Erie Ry to Niagara Falls ; N. Y. C. & H. R. R. to Utica ; U. & B. R. R. R. & Ferry to Brockville. Rate..$27.50

Route No. 11.—U. & B. R. R. R. to Utica ; N. Y. C. & H. R. R. R. to Niagara Falls ; Erie R. R. to Waverly ; L. V. R. R. to Allentown or Bethlehem ; P. & R. or N. P. R. R. to Philadelphia ; Penn. R. R. to Manunka Chunk ; D., L. & W. R. R. to Utica ; U. & B. R. R. to Brockville. Fare from Brockville................................$26.50

Route No. 12.—U. & B. R. R. R. to Utica ; N. Y. C. & H. R. R. R. to New York ; Jersey City Ferry to Jersey

City ; Penn. R. R. to Philadelphia ; P. & R. R. R. to Williamsport ; N. C. R. R. to Canandaigua ; N. Y. C. & H. R. R. R. to Niagara Falls ; N. Y. C. & H. R. R. R. to Utica ; U & B. R. R. to Brockville.

Fare from Brockville........... ....$27.50

Route No. 13.—U. & B. R. R. to Utica ; N. Y. C. & H. R. R. to New York ; Jersey City Ferry to Jersey City ; Penn. R. R. to Philadelphia ; P. W. & B. R. R. to Baltimore ; B. & P. R. R. to Washington ; B. & P. R. R. to Baltimore ; P. W. & B. R. R. to Philadelphia ; Penn. R. R. to New York ; N. Y. C. & H. R. R. R. to Utica ; U. & B. R. R. R. and Ferry to Brockville.

Fare from Brockville.................... ......$27.45

Route No. 14.—U. & B. R. R. R. to Utica ; N. Y. C. & H. R. R. R. to New York ; Jersey City Ferry to Jersey City.   Penn. R. R. to Philadelphia : P., W. & B. R. R. to Baltimore ; B. & P. R. R. fo Washington ; B. & P. R. R. to Baltimore ; P., W. & B. R. R. to Philadelphia ; Penn. R. R. to Manunka Chunk ; D., L. & W R. R. to Utica ; U. & B. R. R. R. to Brockville.

Fare from Brockville.........................$27.10

Tourists north of Brockville can receive return tickets, in connection with Centennial tickets by the Utica & Black River, or Rome and Watertown Roads, as follows, payable in gold :—Ottawa, $3.75 ; Carleton Place, $2.80 ; Smith's Falls, $1.70 ; Perth, $2.40 ; to Brockville. Ottawa to Prescott by St. Lawrence Railway, the same.

NEW YORK CENTRAL RAILWAY.

Of all the great railway lines in America, there is none that affords as much general satisfaction to the travelling public as this road, on account of its railroad facilities, and the excellent time made, under all circumstances.   It costs a trifle more to go to Philadelphia by this route than by cutting " across lots," but the extra expense is well repaid by the absence of numerous changes and delays experienced

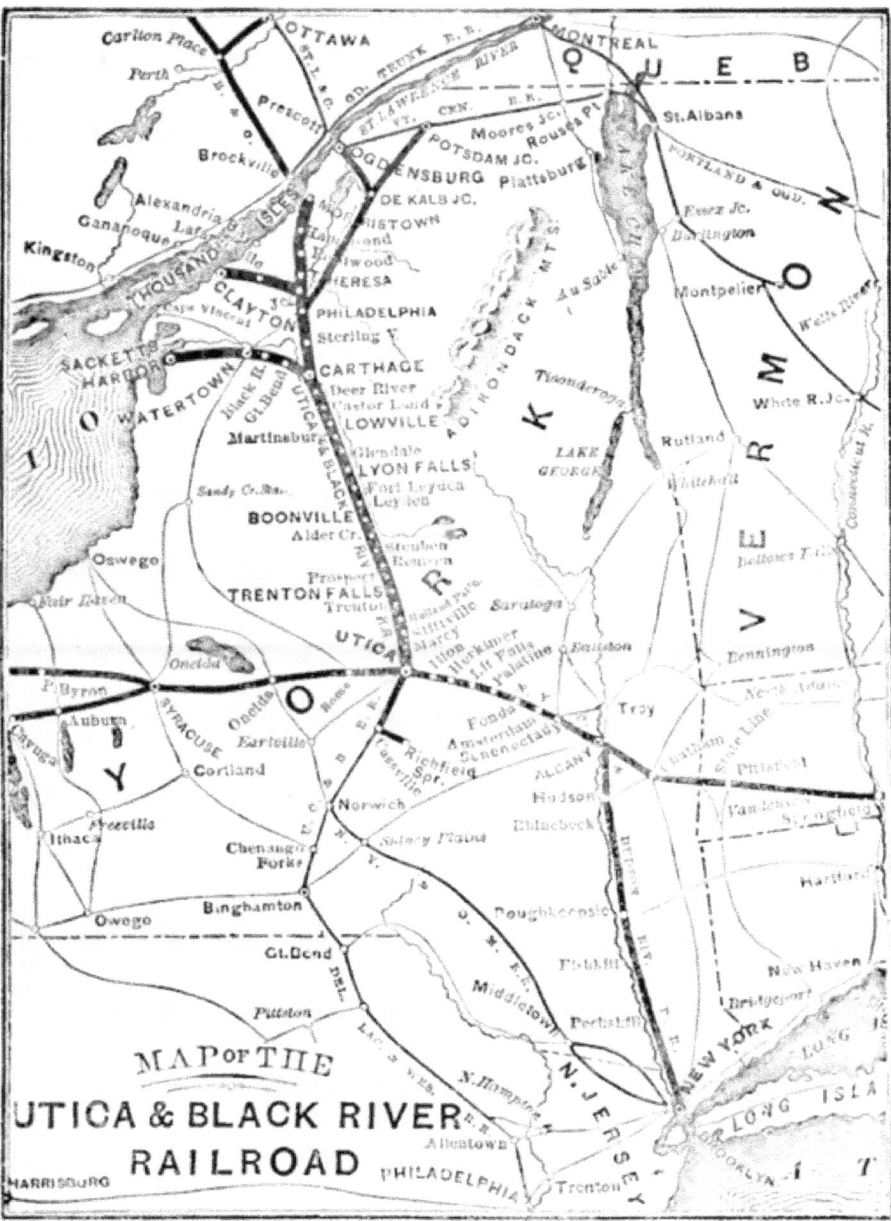

MAP OF THE UTICA & BLACK RIVER RAILROAD

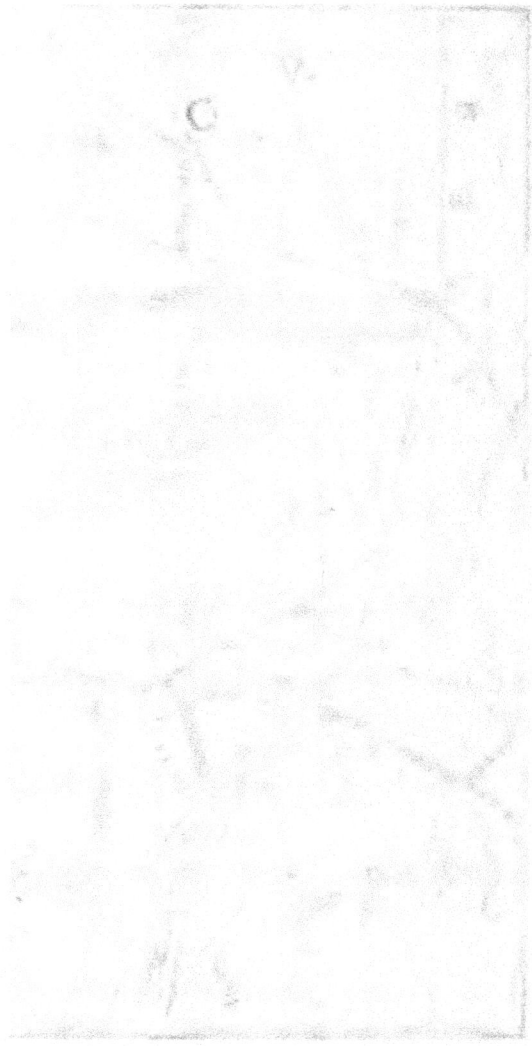

on other roads, and a view of the scenic grandeur afforded by its proximity to the Hudson. Passengers going over other roads connecting with the Central, should manage to make the trip up or down the Hudson by daylight, securing a seat on the right side of the car going down, and the left coming up the river.

Those taking the Atlantic Express, which leaves Niagara Falls at 1:45 p.m., Buffalo, 1:50 p.m., Rochester, 5:10 p.m., Rome, 9:30 p.m., and Utica at 10 p.m., should take the lower berth in a sleeping car, if they are at all fond of scenery. Awakening at Poughkeepsie about daylight, the tourist can push his curtain one side, and feast his eyes with a panorama of nature for one and a half hours, which will ever afterwards remain a bright spot in his memory. We mention this as a special feature of a fast train that makes connections with railways running from our frontier, affords a good nights rest, and lands one in New York at a reasonable hour in the morning.

The passenger unacquainted with sleeping cars will bear in mind that in the hot season the upper berth is the cooler, and also that the choice of berths will sometimes be refused, for one reason or another, but by informing the conductor that your wishes in the matter must be complied with, or you will leave the car, you will generally be accommodated.

Route No. 1.—To Philadelphia via Canandaigua, Elmira and Harrisburg; returning via same route, or via Allentown, Ithaca and Geneva.

Fare.............. .... $16

Route No. 2.—To Philadelphia via Seneca Lake, Watkin's Glen, Elmira and Harrisburg; returning via Harrisburg and Canandaigua, or via Allentown or Bethlehem, Ithaca and Geneva.

Fare....... .... $16

Route No. 3.—To Philadelphia via Canandaigua. Williamsport and Reading; returning via same or any of the routes.

Fare..$16

Route No. 4.—To Philadelphia via any of the above routes, returning via New York City.

Fare..$17

Route No. 5.—To Philadelphia via New York City. returning via New York City.

Fare..$18

The above rates are from Buffalo, Niagara Falls and Suspension Bridge.

GREAT WESTERN RAILWAY.

The following rates are adopted from Suspension Bridge and Buffalo to Philadelphia and return, payable in U. S. currency :—

Route No. 1.—New York Central to Canandaigua ; Northern Central to Williamsport; P. & E. Division to Sunbury; Northern Central to Harrisburg; Pennsylvania to Philadelphia, and return by the same route.

Fare..$16

This route passes through Watkins, but does not allow a trip over Lake Geneva.

Route No. 2.—New York Central or Erie Railway to New York; Pennsylvania to Philadelphia, and returning by the direct line, as mentioned in No. 1.

Fare..$17.00

This route is much preferable to No. 1, as it affords a trip over the best railway in America, with but one change. and beautiful scenery on the return trip. We would advise those who stop at Watkin's to go to the Lake View House on account of the location. The Watkins Glen House is in connection with the Glen, but the tourist will find it much more pleasant at the other hotel on account of its proximity to the Lake, and the charming view afforded from its balconies.

Route No. 3. —New York Central or Erie Railways to New York, Pennsylvania to Philadelphia, returning by Pensylvania to New York, and either the Central or Erie to starting point.

Fare... ....$18.00

Passengers from inland ports, must pay the several amounts annexed to the following places, in Canada funds:—

From St. Catharines, 70 cts. ; from Hamilton, $2.10 ; from Toronto, $3.90 ; from Dundas, $2.35; from Harrisburg, $3.00 ; from Brantford, $3.15 ; from Galt, $3.55 ; from Guelph, $4.30 ; from Elora, $4.45 ; from Listowel, $6.55 ; from Wingham, $7.80 ; from Kincardine, $9.10 ; from Clifford, $6.70 ; from Harriston, $6.40; from Walkerton, $7.35 ; from Paris, $3.55 ; from Woodstock, $4.30 ; from Ingersoll, $4.75 ; from London, $5.65 ; from St. Thomas, $5 80; from Strathroy, $6.45; from Petrolia, $7.95 ; from Glencoe, $6 90; from Bothwell, $7.35.

From Chatham, Detroit and Sarnia, the Centennial rates will be, in U. S. currency, as follows :—

To Philadelphia, **going and** returning by **direct line,** $23.40.

To Philadelphia, **via New York and returning by** direct line, $24.40.

To Philadelphia, **going and returning by** New York. $25.40.

STEAMER NORSEMAN.

Route by Steamer Norseman from Port Hope, Cobourg, Colborne and Brighton, to Philadelphia and return.

Route No. 1.—Route by Northern Central, passing through Rochester, Canandaigua, Watkins, Elmira, Williamsport, and Harrisburg, returning by same route.

Fare..................... $18.40, **American currency.**

Route No. 2.—Route by Rochester, Avon to main line of Erie at Corning, thence by Erie to Jersey City. Pensylvania R. R. to Philadelphia, returning by same route.

Fare.................... .... $18.40, American currency.

Route No. 3.—Route by Rochester, New York Central to New York, Pensylvania to Philadelphia, returning by same route.

Fare...... .... $19.40, American currency.

Passengers purchasing tickets by the Northern Central have the privilege of visiting Baltimore and Washington without further expense. The Norseman leaves Port Hope every morning at 9.40, on the arrival of east and west trains on the Grand Trunk. Passengers can reach Philadelphia via Northern Central at 7.35 next morning, by the Pensylvania, or the Philadelphia & Reading Railways, from Harrisburg, and New York by the New York Central at 7 a.m.

CENTRAL VERMONT RAILWAY.

Route No. 1.—From Montreal via St. Albans, High Gate Springs, Burlington, Troy, New York to Philadelphia and return by same route.

Fare........... .. . . $22.00

Route No. 2.—From Montreal via St. Albans, White River Junction, Springfield, Hartford, New York to Philabelphia, and return by same route.

Fare............ .... $23.75

Route No. 3.—From Montreal via White River Junction, Bellows Falls, So Vernon, New London, and Steamer to New York, Pensylvania R. R. to Philadelphia. Returning by same route.

Fare........ ..... ---- $22.00

Route No. 4.—From Montreal by Route No. 1, returning via Steamers to Boston, and railroad through Lowell, Boston, Concord, and White River Junction.

Fare.. .... $24.50

Route No. 5.—From Montreal via Burlington, Albany, steamers to New York, R. R. to Philadelphia, returning via New Haven. Springfield, South Vernon, and St. Albans.

Fare.. $22.00

Route No. 6.—Montreal to St. Albans, Burlington, C. T. Co. to Ticonderoga, Railway to Saratoga, Albany, New York and Philadelphia, returning by rail to Springfield, Connecticut River to South Vernon, and railroad home.

Fare $23.75

Route No. 7.—From Montreal by Route No. 6, returning by rail through New York, Troy, Rutland and St. Johns

Fare.. $22,00

Route No. 8.—Railroad to Ticonderoga and Baldwins' steamer to Caldwell, stage to Glens Falls, railroad through Albany to Philadelphia. Returning by New York, Troy, State Line, and Rutland.

Fare..... .... $26.75

NEW JERSEY SOUTHERN.

A pleasant and profitable trip from Philadelphia to New York, is on the New Jersey Southern Railway, running from Camden opposite the foot of Market Street. The route passes through Long Branch along the Atlantic Coast to Sandy Hook, from which point steamers run up the Sound to Pier No. 8, New York. Besides affording an opportunity to visit Long Branch and enjoy a walk or a ride on the famous Beach, it presents many points of interest from Sandy Hook up the Sound, such as Forts, Lafayette, Hamilton, Wadsworth and Richmond, besides passing Quarantine, the residence of Judge Brunt, (where Douglas, one of the abductors of Charles Ross, was killed,) Coney Island, and Rockaway Beach. On arriving at New York, walk up to Pier No. 16, and take a car crossing Broadway and every Avenue in the city.

BOARDING HOUSES AND HOTELS.

Under this heading will be found a list of respectable boarding houses, and their rates per day or week. Centennial visitors will find it much more pleasant to engage rooms in advance by mail, which can be done by addressing the proprietors. Instructions are added to each card, showing how to reach the number by street car from the Pensylvania Railway depot.

MERCHANT'S HOTEL.

This popular hotel having accommodations for 800 persons, is situated on 4th street, between Market and Arch, and is one of the oldest Hotels in the city, having been built in the year 1840. It was for many years the headquarters of Southern Politicians, many still making it their home in the city.

It is fitted up with all the latest improvements, such as modern bath rooms, steam elevator &c., &c. To those who delight in visiting historic points, this house has a peculiar interest. Directly in front of it is the old Penn meeting house with capacious grounds, which was to revert to the British Government when vacated for religious purposes. A little to the right rises the spire of Christs Church, which was completed in 1754, and contains the chime of bells which were removed before the British entered the city, and replaced at the close of the revolution.

Directly back of the Hotel rests the remains of Dr. Benjamin Franklin and his wife Debora, marked only by a plain slab with proper inscription. The whole vicinity of the Merchant's, abounds with such points of interest, and attracts many strangers to its capacious quarters.

The present proprietors are Canadians. One of them, L. W. Cass, kept the Royal at Hamilton, and is well known to the travelling public, Mr. S. O. Case, the senior partner is also from **Hamilton**.

The terms are $3.00 per day. For the convenience of visitors to the Exhibition, dinner will be served from 6 till 10 p. m , in addition to the regular dinner from 12 to 3. The dinning room being between two open lots, is the coolest in that part of the city, and has seating room for 300 persons.

Three lines of cars, one on Arch, the first street north, one on Walnut, the first street south, and one passing by the door, go direct to the Exhibition grounds.

To reach this Canadian headquarters from Pensylvania Railway depot, take **Market** street cars to 4th street, and and walk north to hotel ; from Philadelphia & Reading Railway Depot on Callowhill street, take Callowhill street cars going east to 4th, and 4th street cars to the door.

MARBLE TERRACE.

Chestnut street is the 5th Avenue of Philadelphia, and on its upper portion will be found the finest residencies in the city, especially above 34th street. Between 32nd and and 33rd streets stands a colossal building occupying the whole space between the two streets on the south side. It is called Marble Terrace, from the fact that its whole front is composed of Marble, even to the uppermost story.

At 3254, Mrs. DeKalb of Montreal, has opened a boarding house for Canadians, who will find there all the comforts of a home. The rooms are excellently furnished in keeping with what one might expect in such a quarter, and with such surroundings. Each flat is furnished, bath rooms supplied with shower-baths, and hot and cold water, and all the rooms supplied with bells, sounding trumpets etc., **etc.**

It is only one block from the depot of the Pensylvania Railway, and can be reached by walking south on 32nd street, or taking Chestnut street cars. It is open for transient or permanent boarders, and the table will be found first-class, with good attendance. It is convenient to Theatres down town, and Centennial cars pass the door. The Pensylvania University is one block above.

Board per day $3.00, with lunch at noon, and dinner on return from the Exhibition Grounds, only 15 minutes ride by Chestnut street cars.

1776. CENTENNIAL EXPOSITION. 1876.

FULLER HOUSE

Nos. 4031 and 4033 Powelton Avenue, between 40th and 41st Streets,

PHIEADELPHIA.

This First-Class **House was** opened May 10th, 1876. **The** House has every modern convenience, and is furnished with new furniture and bedding. The House will accommodate about seventy-five guests The charge for Board will be from $2 **to $3** per day, **according** to location of room. A reduction made to Permanent Boarders and Parties. **The Fuller House is ten minutes ride** from the Centennial Grounds. Street Cars pass within one-half square of the House to all parts of the city. Guests wishing to reach the House from the Centennial Grounds, take Market Street Cars, at Main Entrance, and stop at Fortieth Street and Powelton Avenue. Guests arriving at Pennsylvania Railroad Depot, 32d and Market Streets, take Market Street Cars going west, and stop at Forty-first Street and Powelton Avenue. Guests arriving at any of the other Depots in the City, can buy an Exchange Ticket, and take the Market Street Cars going west and stop at Forty-first Street and Powelton Avenue. Booms may be secured in advance for any time during the Exposition. Remember the Street and number.

W. H. TOWLE, *Supt.*   S. F. HUNT, *Prop.*

B. C. WHEELER

CHOICE ACCOMMODATIONS

FOR VISITORS TO THE

CENTENNIAL EXPOSITION.

The Large ane Finely Furnished Private Residence,

No. 1428 POPLAR ST.,

PHILADELPHIA,

Has been thrown open for the Reception of Visitors to the Exposition. Having been occupied for years as the home of one of the prominent merchants of our city, and fitted up furnished by him for his own use, the accommodations afforded by this house cannot fail of pleasing those who prefer the quiet of a home, to the bustle of a hotel.

ITS LOCATION IS SUPERIOR,

Being situated in the most eligible section of the city, on a principal street, within half a block of the great thoroughfare—Broad Street—

20 MINUTES DISTANT FROM THE EXPOSITION GROUNDS,

And Easy of Access to and from the lower portions of the city.

Table Strictly First Class.

Special accommodation for small excursion parties. Rooms engaged in advance.

TERMS. - - **$2.50 PER DAY.**

For the accommodation of those wishing it, a plain, portable lunch will be provided, at a small cost, thus avoiding the necessity of an expenditure at the grounds.

Centennial Arrangements.

Fast Time ! Close Connections ! !

Ogdensburg to Philadelphia

IN 16 HOURS VIA

ROME, WATERTOWN & OGDENSBURG R.R.

On and after Monday June 12th, 1876, and until further notice, 3 Express Trains will leave Ogdensburg daily, (Sunday excepted.)

Special New York and Philadelphia Express leaves Ogdensburg at 5 a.m. ; arriving at Syracuse 10:40 a.m. ; Rome 10:45 a.m.; Utica, 11:15 a.m. ; Albany, 2:20 p.m. ; New York 7 p.m ; Philadelphia (via Syracuse) 9 p.m. ; Boston 11 p.m. ; Philadelphia (via New York) 11:40 p.m.

Coaches and Drawing Room Cars run through from Syracuse to Philadelphia without change.

SPECIAL DAY EXPRESS

Leaves Ogdensburg 7:50 a.m. ; arriving at Rome 1:45 p.m. ; Syracuse 2:15 p.m. ; Utica 2:15 p.m. ; Albany 5:25 p.m. ; New York 9.58 p.m ; Philadelphia (via New York) 5 p.m.; Boston 6:15 a. m.

NEW YORK EXPRESS

Leaves Ogdensburg at 2 p.m. ; arriving at Syracuse 7:40 p.m. ; Utica 9:15 p.m. ; Albany 12:40 a.m. ; New York 6:30 a.m. ; Philadelphia (via New York) 10:10 a.m. ; Boston 10 a.m. Sleeping car attached at Watertown to train leaving Ogdensburg at 2 p.m., and run through to New York.

Through tickets to Utica, Albany, New York, Springfield, Boston, and all principal points East and West. Also Centennial Excursion tickets by 18 different routes, can be obtained of Geo. T. Fulford, Agent Brockville, O'Connor & Waller, Agents Ottawa, T. N. Derby, Ogdensburg, and at all the principal ticket offices of this company. Be sure and secure your tickets via Rome, Watertown & Ogdensburg R.R.

The only direct and reliable route to all points East.

H. T. FRARY, Gen'l Ticket Agent.

58

Good Board, nice rooms, every comfort, $2 per day, private family. MRS. BLOVELT, 2144 Master Street. Take Market and 19 St. cars.

Good Board, two nice rooms, every home comfort, Private family, $2 per day. Miss MATHEY'S, 1329 Park Avenue. Take Market and 13th St. cars.

FIRST CLASS BOARD,

Private family, nice parlor, bath, piano, walnut furniture. $1.50 to $2.50 per day, convenient to Exposition, and all places of interest.

N. NOURSE,
No. 1011 Fairmount Avenue.
Take Market and 8th St. cars.

FIRST CLASS BOARD,

Large, airy, well furnished rooms, parlor, piano, bath, and all home comfort. Healthy location, strictly private family. Convenient to Exposition, all places of amusement and interests. $12 to $14 per week.

J. V. BOULBY, 661 north 10th St.
Take Market and 11th St. cars.

GERMANTOWN COTTAGE HOMES.

INDIVIDUALS OR FAMILIES

Intending to visit the Centennial Exhibition to be held at Philadelphia this year, can now engage

Comfortable Sleeping Rooms

And First-Class Board at $2.50 per day. On and after May 1st we will be prepared to entertain a large number of Guests. It will be necessary for visitors to engage rooms at as early a day as possible. Address all Inquiries and Communications to

WM. B. SMITH, Proprietor,
147 East Chelten Avenue, Germantown, Philadelphia, Pa.

59

1776. CENTENNIAL. 1876.

FIRST CLASS BOARDING AND LODGING

AT 1928 & 1930 MT. VERNON ST.,

BY MR. & MRS. E. R. SHEPARD,

(FORMERLY OF BINGHAMPTON, N. Y.)

We take pleasure in being able to inform our many friends and acquaintances that we have secured the two above mentioned communicating, four story, large and handsomely furnished residences, admirably arranged and located, for a pleasant, cool, and quiet HOME during the Centennial Exposition. The location has few (if any) equals in the city, in points of general conveniences; being situated about midway between the business centre, Independence Hall, places of amusement, and the Centennial grounds. Especially so in its accessibility to Fairmount Park and the Exhibition Building, by steam and horse cars, and boats on the Schuylkill. Four lines of horse cars within a block, for all parts of the city, and two depots for steam cars within a half mile, also a line of Centennial Coaches, 25c. fares, have a stand one block distant. By walking a short distance at each end of the route, a delightful ride on the river takes you to the grounds ; or, if preferred, it will be found a very pleasant walk of two miles through the Park. The LOCATION possesses the advantage of being in a first-class neighborhood, on high grounds,—no mosquitoes—cool, and quiet ; no cars passing the door, yet Mount Vernon street is one of the popular drives or approach to the main entrance of Fairmount Park, less than half a mile distant. Further, just within and beyond the Park entrance, are the Fairmount Water Works, steamboat landing, music pavillion etc. Everything that personal attention, good board, attentive waiters, and a two years residence in Philadelphia, can do to make it pleasant for our guests, will be done. Terms, with full board, $2, $2.50 and $3, per day, according to room and accommodations. " A good safe in the office."

E. R. SHEPARD, Manager.
No. 1930 Mount Vernon St., Philadelphia, Pa.

Good board, nice front rooms, private family, $1 to $1.50 a day, or $6 to $8 a week, No, 2327 Jefferson St. Take Market and 19th St. cars.

Good Board, first-class house, highest location, near Girard College, $2 to 2.50 per day. Cars direct to Main Exhibition building, No. 1431 N. 18th St. Take Market and 18th St. cars.

Pleasant house, good board, convenient to Exposition and all parts of the city, Healthy location, $2 per day, MRS. H. HICKS, 1114 Columbia Avenue. Take Market and 11th St. cars.

Good board, nice rooms, convenient to Exposition and all places of interest, $1 to $2 a day, private family. Mrs. ANNA DYCE, 1309 Fairmount Avenue. Take Market St. car to 8th St., then the Fairmount Avenue car.

MRS. E. BROWN,

422, No. 7th street, 1 large room for a party, two communicating rooms, nicely furnished in 2nd story. Two communicating rooms in 3rd story. Rooms $1 per day without board.

Market Street cars to 8th street, north to Noble street, Noble to 7th, a few doors to the right.

Large, airy, nicely furnished rooms, first-class board, healthy location, convenient to all parts of the city. Cars direct to Exposition. $1.50 to $2.50 per day, $10 to $15 per week.

E. C. BULLOCK,
2303 Delancy Place.

Take Market and 20th St. cars.

FIRST CLASS BOARD,

$1.50 to $2 per day, $8 to $11 per week, large, airy, well furnished rooms. convenient to Exposition and all places of interest and amusement.

THOS. IRVING,
1804 Catharine St.

Take Market and 17th St. Cars.

Good board, home comforts, convenience, healthy location, convenient to all points of city, $1.50 to $2 per day. MRS. CRESS, 1218 Mt. Vernon St. Take Market and 11th St. cars.

Good board, home comforts, convenient to Exposition and all places of interest, healthy location, $2 per day. P. FLEMING, No. 1318 Girard Ave. Take Market and 15th St. cars.

FIRST CLASS BOARD,

Elegantly furnished rooms, parlor, bath, piano, gas, private family, street cars direct to Exposition, convenient to all points of city, $1.50 to $2 per day.

MRS. M. A. WHITBY,
1530 Christian St.

Take Market and 17th St. cars.

FIRST CLASS BOARD.

Large, airy, well furnished rooms, parlor, bath and all home comforts, healthy location, strictly private family. Convenient to Exposition and all points of city, $2 per day.

D. M. BORING,
2015 Poplar St.

Take Market and 19th St. cars.

FIRST CLASS BOARD,

Nicely furnished rooms, every home comfort and convenience, nice parlor, convenient to Exposition and all places of interest, $1.50 per day.

MRS. M. COXEY,
3829 Haverford Ave., West Phila.

Take Chestnut St. and Lancaster Ave. cars.

FIRST CLASS BOARD,

Nicely furnished rooms, every home comfort and convenience, nice parlor, convenient to Exposition and all places of interest, $1.50 per day.

MRS. H. F. WILSON,
1906 Poplar St.

Take Market and 19th St. cars.

Good board, home comforts, private family, convenient to Exposition and all places of interest, $1.25 to $2 a day. WM. JAMES, 1330 Parish St. Take Market and 15th St. cars.

Good board, nice rooms, private family, home comforts convenient to Exposition and all places of interest, $1 to $2 per day. MRS. M. A. COATS, S. E. corner 18th and Mt. Vernon Sts. Take Market and 18th St. cars.

Large, airy, well furnished rooms, with or without board. Cars pass the door direct to and from Exposition, and all places of interest, private. MRS. S. PARK, 1808, Girard Avenue. Take Market & 19th St car from P.R.R. Depot.

Good board, large, airy, nicely furnished rooms, private family. Convenient to Exposition and all places of interest. $2 to $2.50 a day. MRS. WILES, 3113 Spring Garden St., near Penyslvania Railroad Depot.

GOOD BOARD,

Nicely furnished rooms, private family, high and healthy, cenvenient to Exposition and places of interest, $1.50 to $2 per day.

J. J. HAMAN,
1829 Sharswood St

Take Market and 19th St. cars.

GOOD BOARD,

Nicely furnished rooms, private family, home comforts and conveniences, $1.50 to $2 per day.

E. F. JUDSON,
3229 Sansom St. Mansard Square, West Philadelphia one square south of Penn. R. R. depot.

MRS. HASWELL

904 Pine Street. An elegantly furnished house, on the south side, three large rooms in the 2nd story, four well furnished rooms in 3rd story. Only four squares from the Continental Hotel, and convenient to Theatres. Take Market street cars to 10th and 10th to Pine.

E. P. McGEE,

North West corner of 10th & Cherry Streets, entrance No. 1001 Cherry St. Contains 13 rooms splendidly furnished and inspected by the agent of the Guide. Beds furnished with Spring Mattrasses, very desirable location within one-half square of cars running direct to Centennial grounds. Market street cars to 10th, thence to Cherry. Rooms, supper, and breakfast, $2 to $4 per day, according to room.

ROBERT CARTER,

924 Pine Street, 3 streets south of Market, in the centre of city. Part of 4 stories, 10 rooms, some of them single. Black walnut furniture; only three squares from Theaters and large Hotels. Board $2 to $2.50 per day, according to room. Reduction for over 1 week.

Market street cars to 10th, tenth to Pine.

1732 CHESTNUT STREET,

First class four story Brown Stone house. All modern improvements on principal street of the city, convenient to all places of interest and amusement. Cars pass the door to Exhibition ground.

Take Chestnut Street cars from depot direct to the house.

www.ingramcontent.com/pod-product-compliance
Lightning Source LLC
Chambersburg PA
CBHW021519090426
42739CB00007B/685